FOR CAT LOVERS
EVERYWHERE:

Blessed are those who love cats,
for they shall never be lonely.

To:

_____

From:

_____

The Proverbial Cat

RONNIE
SELLERS
PRODUCTIONS
PORTLAND, MAINE

Published by Ronnie Sellers Productions, Inc.

Copyright ©2006 Sydney Hauser

Publishing Director: Robin Haywood
Managing Editor: Mary Baldwin
Assistant Production Editor: Kathy Fisher

81 West Commercial Street, Portland, Maine 04101
For ordering information:
Toll-free: 1-800-625-3386
Fax: (207) 772-6814
Visit our Web site: www.rsvp.com
E-mail: rsp@rsvp.com

ISBN 10: 1-56906-974-3
ISBN 13: 978-1-56906-974-5

Text credits appear on pages 110.

Printed and bound in China.

The Proverbial Cat

A friend is someone who listens with the heart.

Feline Inspirations by Sydney Hauser

efore a cat will condescend
　　To treat you as a trusted friend,
Some little token of esteem
Is needed, like a dish of cream.

In ancient times, cats were worshipped as gods. They have never forgotten this.

Is·it·dinner·yet?

ats seem to go on the principle that it never does any harm to ask for what you want.

There are no ordinary cats.

I saw the most beautiful cat today. It was sitting by the side of the road, its two front feet neatly and graciously together. Then it gravely swished around its tail to completely and snugly encircle itself. It was so fit and beautifully neat, that gesture, and so self-satisfied — so complacent.

Joy is a little fur bundle.

Sandpaper kisses
on a cheek or a chin.
That is the way
for a day to begin!
Sandpaper kisses
a cuddle and purr.
I have an alarm clock
that's covered in fur!

ats are absolute individuals, with their own ideas about everything, including the people they own.

14

Home is where the cat is.

Cats sleep
Anywhere,
Any table,
Any chair,
Top of piano,
Window ledge,
In the middle,
On the edge,
Open drawer,
Empty shoe,

Anybody's
Lap will do,
Fitted in a
Cardboard box,
In the cupboard
With your frocks.
Anywhere!
They don't care!
Cats sleep
Anywhere.

The best things in life aren't things.

If there is one
spot of sun
s p i l l i n g

onto the floor,
a cat will find it
and soak it up.

Joy is in little things...
a little cat, a little book,
time spent reading in a cozy nook.

I put down my book, *The Meaning
of Zen*, and see the cat smiling into
her fur as she delicately combs it
with her rough pink tongue. Cat,
I would lend you this book to study
but it appears you have already read
it. She looks up and gives me her full
gaze. Don't be ridiculous, she purrs,
I wrote it.

CAT PEOPLE ARE DIFFERENT
to the extent that they
generally are not
conformists. How
could they be, with
a cat running their lives?

A cat has absolute honesty; Human Beings, for one reason or another, may hide their feelings but a cat does not.

Ernest Hemingway

The cat goes out
And the cat comes back
And no one can follow
Upon her track.
She knows where she's going
She knows where she's been,
All we can do
Is to let her in.

Cats make purrfect friends.

Tattoo was the mother of Pinkle Purr,
A ridiculous kitten with silky fur.
And little black Pinkle grew and grew
Till he got as big as the big Tattoo.
And all he did he did with her.
"Two friends together," says Pinkle Purr.

A HOME WITHOUT A CAT,
and a well-fed, well-petted,
and properly revered cat
may be a perfect home,
perhaps, but how can it
prove its title?

There are people who reshape the world by force or argument, but the cat just lies there, dozing, and the world quietly reshapes itself to suit his comfort and convenience.

A friend is someone who listens with the heart.

Gentle eyes that see so much,
Paws that have the quiet touch,
Purrs to signal "all is well"
And show more love than words could tell.
Graceful movements touched with pride,
A calming presence by our side
A friendship that takes time to grow
Small wonder why we love them so.

Happy owner . . .
happy cat . . .

True friendship is feline companionship.

If you love something, set it free...
if it doesn't come back,
it was never meant to be,
if it does return, love it forever.

believe cats to
be spirits come to
Earth. A cat, I am sure,
could walk on a cloud
without coming through.

Though I'm
only human,
make me worthy
of my kitty!

You never really leave
a place you love.

It is in a cat's
eyes that the
magic resides.

Worthy of its
affection, a cat
will be your friend,
but never your slave.

To love something
is to give it
room to grow.

Take comfort in the little things.

 Wisdom
comes to
those who
live with
both feet
(or all paws)
on the ground.

*Of all animals,
the cat alone
attains to the
contemplative life.*

Time with a cat puts life's problems into perspective.

Sydney Hauser

A cat, though independent, has a way of letting you know that without you life just wouldn't be worthwhile.

A cat can
purr its
way out
of *anything*.

To·err·is·human,
to·purr·is·feline.

Love does not consist of gazing at each other, but in looking in the same direction together.

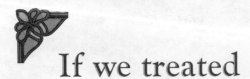

If we treated
everyone we
meet with the
same affection
we bestow upon
our favorite
cat, they, too,
would purr.

Cats are intended
to teach us
that not everything
in nature has a
purpose.

*A kitten is
the most
irresistible
comedian in
the world.
Its wide open
eyes gleam
with wonder
and mirth.*

Better·to·feed·one·cat·than·many·mice.

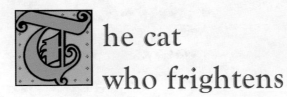he cat
who frightens
the mice away is
as good as the
cat who eats them.

Cats are kindly masters,
just so long as you
remember your place!

Cats don't like change without their consent.

I purr... therefore, I am.

Louder he purrs, and louder,
in one glad hymn of praise
for all the night's adventures,
for quiet, restful days.
Life will go on forever,
with all that cat can wish:
warmth and the glad procession
of fish and milk and fish.

Blessed are
those who love
cats, for they
shall never be
lonely.

We are given memories so we can have roses in December.

The fog
comes
in on
little
cat
feet.

There has never been a cat
Who couldn't calm me down
By walking slowly
Past my chair.

The ideal of calm exists in a sitting cat.

Jules Reynard

A cat's hearing apparatus
is built to allow the
human voice to
go easily in one ear
and out the other.

When the tea is
brought at five o'clock,
And all the neat curtains
are drawn with care,
The little black cat with
bright green eyes
is suddenly purring there.

The best
things in life
aren't things

A big dust ball is the kitten.

The cat was created
when the lion
s n e e z e d.

How we behave
toward cats
determines our
status in heaven.

Animals are such agreeable friends, they ask no questions, they pass no criticisms.

– George Eliot

A meow
massages
the heart.

*Who among us
hasn't envied a cat's
ability to ignore the
cares of daily life and
to relax completely?*

A home·without·a·cat· is·like·a·garden· without·flowers.

Happy is
the home
with at
least one
cat.

Since each of us
is blessed with only
one life, why not
live it with a cat?

God made the Cat so that we might know the pleasure of embracing the Lion.

The heart which gives
freely is never lonely.

hen you're
special to a cat,
you're special indeed . . .
she brings to you
the gift of her preference
of you, the sight of you,
the sound of your voice,
the touch of your hand.

Cat hair on the bedspread,
Cat hair on the chair.
Cat hair in the casserole,
Cat hair EVERYWHERE!
Cat hair on my best coat,
Even on the mouse!
You live and eat and breathe cat hair,
When cats live in your house.

ats·are·connoisseurs
·of·comfort. James Herriott

No matter how much cats fight, there always seems to be plenty of kittens.

Abraham Lincoln

Who could believe
such pleasure from
a wee ball o' fur?

It is impossible to keep a straight face in the presence of one or more kittens.

The smallest of felines is a **masterpiece**

Leonardo da Vinci

The Best and most beautiful things must be felt with the heart.

Helen Keller

Which is more beautiful:
feline movement or
feline stillness?

*Our perfect companions
never have fewer
than four feet.*

*W*ho can believe
there is no soul
behind those luminous eyes. *Theophile Gautier*

Feelings are·everywhere, be·gentle·

There is, indeed, no single quality of the cat that humans could not emulate to their advantage.

The cat always
leaves a mark
on his friend.

Friendship is the inexpressible comfort of feeling safe with a person having neither to weigh thoughts nor measure words.

George Eliot

The phrase "domestic cat" is an oxymoron.

I'm only a cat,
and I stay in my place . . .
Up there on your chair,
on your bed, or your face!
I'm only a cat,
and I don't finick much . . .
I'm happy with cream
and anchovies and such!
I'm only a cat,
and we'll get along fine . . .
As long as you know
I'm not yours . . . you're all mine!

Way down deep,
we're all motivated
by the same urges.
Cats have the courage
to live by them.

THOU ART THE GREAT CAT,
the avenger of the gods,
and the judge of words,
and the president of the
sovereign chiefs and the
governor of the holy
circle; thou art indeed
. . . the Great Cat.

By associating with the cat, our lives only become richer.

The cat and its housekeeping staff reside here.

*In a cat's
eyes,
all things
belong
to cats.*

Cats are a
mysterious
kind of folk.
There is more
passing in their
minds than we
are aware of.

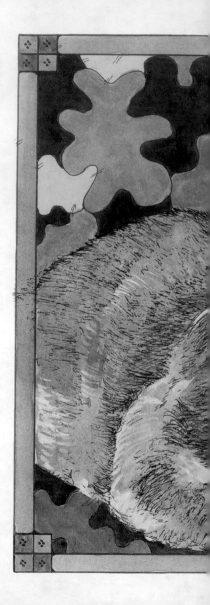

Credits

p. 6, ©T. S. Eliot; p. 9, ©Joseph Wood Krutch; p. 11, ©Mary Morrow Lindburgh; p. 13 author unknown; p. 14, ©John Dingman; p. 17, ©Eleanor Farjeon; p. 19, ©Jean Asper-McIntosh; p. 21, ©Dilys Laing; p. 22, ©Louis J. Camuti, DVM; p. 24, ©Marchette Chute; p. 27, ©A. A. Milne; p. 28, Samuel Clemens; p. 30, ©Allen and Ivy Dodd; p. 33 author unknown; p. 34 Chinese proverb; p. 37, Jules Verne; p. 38 author unknown; p. 41, ©Arthur Symons; p. 42, Theophile Gautier; p. 45 Lizzie Stewart; p. 46, ©Andrew Lang; p. 49, ©Sharon Lundblad; p. 50, ©Donna McCrohan; p. 53,©Martin Buxbaum; p. 55, ©Agnes Repplier; p. 57 German proverb; p. 58, ©Paul Gray; p. 61, ©Alexander Gray; p. 62 author unknown; p. 65, ©Carl Sandburg; p. 66, ©Rod McKuen; p. 69, ©Stephen Baker; p. 70, ©Harold Monro; p. 73 Arabian proverb; p. 74, ©Robert A. Heinlein; p. 77, ©Stuart McMillan; p. 78, ©Karen Brademeyer; p. 81 Italian proverb; p. 82, ©Robert Stearns; p. 85, ©Leonore Fleisher; p. 86 author unknown; p. 89 Irish saying; p. 90, ©Cynthia E. Varnado; p. 93, ©Elizabeth Hamilton; p. 94, ©Sidonie-Gabrielle Colette; p. 97, ©Carl Van Vechten; p. 98 Aesop; p. 101 author unknown; p. 103, ©Jim Davis; p. 104 inscription on the Royal Tombs at Thebes; p. 107 English proverb; p. 108 Sir Walter Scott.